T0198836

Melody Dee

We Are All Great in Our Own Way
(Somos Todos Grandiosos En Nuestra Propia Forma)

DENYS LUCIANO
Illustrated by Angel De La Pena

To order additional copies of this book, contact:
Xlibris
844-714-8691
www.Xlibris.com
Orders@Xlibris.com

ISBN: Softcover   979-8-3694-0144-6
       EBook   979-8-3694-0143-9

Print information available on the last page

Rev. date: 06/20/2023

Melody Dee

We Are All Great in Our Own Way

(Somos Todos Grandiosos En Nuestra Propia Forma)

Acknowledgments

To my son, Liam Abreu (Liam Smart). He is my inspiration and motivation for everything that I do.

I want to thank my mother for always being there for my son and me. Thanks to my father for inheriting his talents.

To my brothers, I love you both.

To my mentor, father, and friend, Giovanni Zambrano, thank you for teaching me work ethic and excellence in everything that I do.

To Karina Lascano, a dear friend and also mentor. She makes me grow by exposing me to new things. Thank you for always believing in me and my potential.

Thank you, family and close friends who are my support system. They encourage me to be a better person every day.

Thanks to my Precious Steps and Precious Steps Too Preschool family. I truly appreciate you all.

Special thanks to those friends that are always supporting my projects and ideas, you are very appreciated and I am thankful to have you in my life. Luis Herrera, Manuel A. Disla, Sayra Marte, Dorka Esther, Eric E. De La Cruz, Mariana de Leon, and Haydee Ramirez, it is amazing to know I can count on you.

For those that are gone but forever in my heart, my grandparents, I carry a piece of you wherever I'll go.

When you think you are not intelligent enough, you must know that there are nine types of intelligence, not just one, not just a form of being intelligent. Don't let a grade define you and know how great and unique you are. You must work on all the subjects, and do the best that you can, but just be aware that you are better at some things than others.

Cuando pienses que no eres lo suficientemente inteligente, debes de saber que hay nueve tipos de inteligencia, no solo una forma de ser inteligente. No dejes que una calificación te defina. Debes de trabajar en todas tus materias y hacer lo mejor que puedas, pero debes de saber que eres mejor en algunas cosas que otras.

The first intelligence that I will introduce is called musical intelligence (sound and music smart). The people that have this intelligence are very sensitive to sounds. Musical intelligence enables you to recognize, reproduce, create, and understand music.

Most popular professions for musical intelligence are composers, conductors, musicians, vocalists, music teachers, and vocal coaches.

La primera inteligencia de la cual te quiero hablar es la inteligencia musical (Sonido y Música)

Las personas que tienen esta inteligencia son muy sensibles a los sonidos. La inteligencia musical te permite reconocer, reproducir, crear y entender la música.

Las profesiones más populares para este tipo de inteligencia son: compositores, conductores, músicos, vocalistas, profesores de música, y entrenadores de vocalistas.

Naturalist intelligence (nature smart) is the ability to understand living things, such as plants, animals, and insects, also the weather, rivers, and everything associated with nature and all living things around us.

The popular professions related to this intelligence are biologist, veterinarian, gardener, scientist, and meteorologist.

La inteligencia naturalista (Inteligencia Natural) Es la habilidad de entender todo lo que tiene vida como las plantas, animales, insectos, además del tiempo, los ríos, y todo lo relacionado con el medio ambiente y los seres vivos a nuestro alrededor.

Las profesiones más populares son: biólogos, veterinarios, científicos, y meteorólogos.

Logical-mathematical intelligence (number/reasoning) is the ability to calculate, quantify, and consider propositions and hypotheses. The people who possess this intelligence are very good with numbers and at solving problems.

Popular professions related to this intelligence are mathematicians, scientists, detectives, and math teachers.

La inteligencia lógica matemática (Números/ razonamiento) es la capacidad de calcular, cuantificar, considerar proposiciones e hipótesis. Las personas que poseen esta inteligencia son muy buenas con los números y resolviendo problemas.

Las profesiones más populares relacionadas con esta inteligencia son: matemáticos, científicos, detectives y profesores de matemática.

Existential intelligence (life smart) gives us the ability to look deep in ourselves and question the meaning of life as well as to understand topics relating to mankind's existence.

Popular professions related to this intelligence are scientists, philosophers, and theologians.

Esta inteligencia nos da la capacidad para mirar profundamente en nosotros mismos y cuestionar el significado de la vida. También para entender los temas relacionados con la existencia de la humanidad.

Las profesiones populares con esta inteligencia son: científicos, filósofos y teólogos.

Interpersonal intelligence (people smart) is the ability to understand and interact with others in a positive way. This intelligence helps you understand people and their feelings and attitude. It involves effective verbal and nonverbal communication.

Popular professions related to this intelligence are teachers, social workers, actors, and politicians.

Inteligencia interpersonal (La inteligencia de personas). Es la capacidad de entender e interactuar con los demás de una manera positiva. Esta inteligencia te ayuda a entender a las personas, sus sentimientos y actitudes. Implica una comunicación verbal y no-verbal efectiva.

Las profesiones populares relacionadas a esta

inteligencia son: profesores, trabajadores sociales, actores y políticos.

Bodily-kinesthetic intelligence (body smart) is the capacity to manipulate objects and use a variety of physical skills. This intelligence involves the sense of timing in perfection of skills through mind and body union.

Popular professions related to this intelligence are surgeons, dancers, acrobats, and athletes.

La inteligencia Kinestésica corporal (inteligencia corporal) es la capacidad de manipular objetos y usar una variedad de habilidades físicas. Esta inteligencia implica el sentido del tiempo en la perfección de las habilidades a través de la unión de mente y cuerpo.

Las profesiones populares relacionadas con esta inteligencia son: cirujanos, bailarines, atletas y acróbatas

Linguistic intelligence (word smart) allows us to understand the order and meaning of words. Linguistic intelligence is the ability to think words and to use the language to express ourselves verbally and nonverbally when writing.

Popular professions related to this intelligence are writers, poets, novelists, and public speakers.

Inteligencia lingüística (inteligencia de palabras) nos permite entender el orden y el significado de las palabras. La inteligencia lingüística es la capacidad de pensar en palabras y usar el lenguaje para expresarnos de forma verbal y no verbal al escribir.

Intrapersonal intelligence (self-smart) gives the capacity to understand oneself and our own thoughts and feelings. This intelligence helps us appreciate ourselves and our human conditions. These people are very aware of their own feelings and are self-motivated.

Popular professions related to this intelligence are psychologists, philosophers, researchers, and spiritual leaders.

Inteligencia intrapersonal (auto inteligencia). Es la capacidad de entenderse a uno mismo y nuestros propios pensamientos y sentimientos. Esta inteligencia nos ayuda a apreciarnos a nosotros mismos y nuestras condiciones humanas. Estas personas son muy conscientes de sus propios sentimientos y se automotivan.

Las profesiones populares relacionadas con esta inteligencia son: psicólogos, investigadores, y líderes espirituales.

Spatial intelligence (visual intelligence) is the ability to successfully perceive the insight from visual data. People with spatial intelligence have the ability of mental imagery, spatial reasoning, graphic and artistic skills, and active imagination.

Popular professions related to this intelligence are sailors, architects, pilots, and graphic designers.

La inteligencia espacial (Inteligencia visual) es la capacidad de percibir con éxito las informaciones visuales. Las personas con esta inteligencia espacial tienen la capacidad de las imágenes mentales, razonamiento espacial, las habilidades gráficas y artísticas y la imaginación activa.

Las profesiones populares relacionadas con esta inteligencia son: marineros, arquitectos, pilotos y diseñadores gráficos.

The key to being great is knowing yourself and your abilities. Once you know your strengths, you have an advantage. I hope this information will help you throughout your life. And remember to work on your intelligence and develop it until you become a master to put it at the service of the world.

La clave para ser grande es conocerte a ti mismo, y tus habilidades, una vez conoces tus fortalezas tienes una ventaja. Espero que esta información te ayude durante toda tu vida. Y recuerda trabajar en tu inteligencia y desarrollarla hasta que te conviertas en un maestro para ponerlo al servicio del mundo.

About the Author

Denys Luciano was born in the city of Miami, Florida, on a sunny day on July 8, 1988. Her parents are originally from the Dominican Republic. She was brought there at the age of four with her two brother, where she was raised and began her first years of school. At the age eleven, she returned to the city of Miami where she continued her education.

Denys began to write poems as early as age eleven, she returned to the city of Miami where she continued her education.

When she turned sixteen, she went back to the Dominican Republic. There she met her best friend, Dee M. Fabre, who introduced her to the world of music. He was amazed with her songs and how easy t was for her to perform in front of people. Moments after, she was offered to be in a band as s backup singer. She was a part of the band for a couple years.

Printed in the United States
by Baker & Taylor Publisher Services